INTRODUCTION

Noise is a collection of short stories and poems set in the vibrant city of Rio de Janeiro, in the South East of Brazil. The suburbs chosen to be the scenario for the stories and poems in this book have something significant about them that makes it right for the story. Not every suburb is displayed in the book, but the ones I have spent most of my childhood, my teenage years, and some years of my adulthood before migrating to Australia in 2008.

Noise is a work of fiction. It is not based on or linked to my personal life in any way. Creative writers tend to connect their hearts to the stories they write. But when they are set to write fiction, stories are created from their imagination. Simple as that.

The photographs used in this book were taken by my father Gustavo Raed who lives in Rio de Janeiro, by my husband Roger Salisbury and by myself when we were visiting the city. The photographs give a sense of imagery to the stories.

A LITTLE HISTORY OF RIO

Rio de Janeiro is an electrifying seaside city of Brazil, famous for its 38m Christ the Redeemer statue on the top of Corcovado Mountain, for Copacabana and Ipanema beaches, and for the Sugarloaf Mountain, with cable cars travelling to its hilltop. The city is also known for the *Carnaval*, the most exciting annual festival that exhibits parade floats, musicians and samba dancers dressed in flamboyant costumes.

Rio de Janeiro has been one of Brazil's most popular tourist destinations for decades. It is the most visited city in the Southern Hemisphere. Its lively centre is packed with culture and a rich sense of history and heritage. This makes for an unforgettable place for visitors from all over the world. Rio, as it is usually known, is the second largest city in Brazil and the third largest metropolis in the whole continent of South America.

Rio is hot and humid for most of the year, and the rain is expected between December and March. The coastal suburbs benefit from the cool breeze from the Atlantic Ocean. The landscape and vegetation in and around the city are marvellous, and offer a visual indulgence that has inspired authors and screenwriters from all over the world to write about the 'marvellous city'.

NOISE

COLLECTION OF SHORT STORIES AND
POEMS SET IN RIO DE JANEIRO

ALESSANDRA SALISBURY

Print information available on the last page.

Rev. date: 06/25/2019

To order additional copies of this book, contact:
Xlibris
1-800-455-039
www.xlibris.com.au
Orders@Xlibris.com.au

THE RETURN

(Ipanema – South of Rio - 1990)

Mariana sat on the warm white sand near the water's edge of Ipanema beach, the heart of Rio de Janeiro, where she grew up and where from she moved out about four years ago. She looked out over the Atlantic Ocean, feeling the fresh breeze messing up her long brunette curls. With eyes shut, she felt the sun's warmth. Ipanema beach was hers and Rafael's once, their ideal spot, where they used to hang out, drink, smoke marijuana, enjoy each other's company, and talk about their life together.

Ipanema beach has a unique picture with the Vidigal slums mountain on its right end perfectly accommodating the sunset every afternoon; and on its left end, the Arpoador surf break point shapes out the seashore in a picturesque arc. Mariana was back in that place and she remembered the last time she had been there. She had married Rafael on that beach five years ago, on the last night of Carnaval, which they absolutely loved. They used to perform in the Parade at Ipanema beach every year since High School, where they first met and fell in love. The Carnaval had to be part of their wedding celebration. And so, had Ipanema, where they were locals.

On their wedding day, the Parade had passed through Ipanema beach, after midday, just before Mariana got ready for the ceremony. Dressed in a white flowing dress, she walked down the made-up sand aisle among shells and flowers. Rafael was dressed in khaki pants and in a loose linen white shirt that contrasted with his tan skin. His blonde hair was slightly ruffled and his green eyes showed adoration as he looked at Louise walking down to him. They smiled and held their shaking hands. Even before the celebrant started, they were already whispering their vows to each other.

After the ceremony, they headed to one of Rafael's friend's apartment across from the beach for their party. Friends and family were dressed in Carnaval costumes - bright colours clothing, feathers and masks - so usual to the *cariocas*. It was an authentic wedding party, exactly the way they had dreamed of. Everything was perfect, so they had thought then. Towards the end of the party, Rafael announced the Parade was about the come back to Ipanema for its last run and they all decided to dance through it. Mariana and Rafael, and their friends joined the Carnaval down the street. Lots of happy, loud people were having a blast turning the Parade into a hectic event. As the crowd moved forward, bumping shoulders and partying, Mariana lost sight of Rafael. She kept dancing while looking for him. Everyone seemed too crazy and too high to know where Rafael had gone. She left the Parade, walked back to the apartment and waited for him to come back.

However, Rafael never made it back. No one knew or saw anything. She contacted the police who looked for him for two weeks, and nothing! Rafael was listed as a missing person and they opened up an investigation. Mariana searched Rafael's phone and found out contact numbers linked to drug trafficking but she deleted them before handing the phone to the police. She knew some of his junkie friends who used to buy cocaine from him, but she didn't tell the police as she was afraid for Rafael's life.

One year later, she was still looking for him without any luck. So, she gave up on finding him and moved out from Rio to Torres, a small town on the South of Brazil, to start over a calm, totally different life. Torres was cold, its only beach wasn't as pretty and meaningful as Ipanema's. The locals didn't celebrate Carnaval. Her life went on, she got a job and started dating her new boss, Tom, an Englishman from Manchester who had recently moved to Brazil.

Four years to the day, for the sake of her sister's first childbirth, Mariana came back to Ipanema. She was sitting on that beach, thinking about how things had turned out for her. A man was standing under the coconut tree, watching her. His eyes were captured by her sitting there, alone, facing the ocean. He walked slowly towards her. Mariana sensed the man approaching. She felt extremely calm about it. He got down on his knees right behind her back and whispered.

"*Bom dia*, Mari… please, don't say anything. Just listen…"

Mariana turned around. "Rafael!" She gasped, barely able to speak.

"I never stopped loving you…" He said it straight after her.

"*Meu Deus*!" She stood up and went in shock, fell back over, and passed out. Rafael tried to wake her up shaking her body gently and kissing her lips.

"Please, forgive me… Wake up," he tried again, but she was still unconscious.

He picked her up and took her to the beach emergency post where paramedics took care of her. When she woke up, they told her a man had brought her there and left. Mariana called Tom to pick her up. He was at her sister's house waiting for her. Mariana told Tom she must have fainted from the long exposure to the sun.

It was Carnaval time again and Mariana's friends were going to the street Parade in Ipanema. Mariana felt she shouldn't join them as Tom didn't like Carnaval at all. He wasn't born in Rio. He never understood the festivity during summer time. He didn't like the beach, neither the heat. He never got how *cariocas* would tan at the beach all day long, would eat, drink, talk, and watch the sunset. Then, they would keep on partying, still in their sexy bikinis, walking straight to bars across from the beach to finish their day drinking a tasty *caipirinha*. Tom didn't belong to that culture. He hated *caipirinha*! However, he knew how much she loved Carnaval and how important was for her to join her friends as she was in Rio for only that weekend. So, he said yes and she went.

During the Parade, Mariana set herself free enjoying the Carnaval like the old days. She had a lot to drink and felt her head spinning. Dancing with heaps of other *carnavalescos*, and being dragged by the crowd, she tripped over Rafael's foot, and almost fell on him. He smiled at her and held her hand. He loved seeing her drunk, looking free and euphoric, like they used to be when they were together. She looked at him and laughed.

"*Oi* ghost! I hope you leave me alone!" She turned away from him and kept dancing the samba, ahead with the crowd. He came behind her and held her waist.

"Mari! I have so much to tell you. Let's get out of here and talk," Rafael insisted but she didn't seem interested.

"I hope you find the light, Rafael… There is nothing here for you anymore! Rest in peace." She laughed while being dragged away from him. Rafael wasn't satisfied. He grabbed her arm, and pulled her back close to him, away from the crowd.

"Listen! I had loads of money in debt because of the drugs. I couldn't risk your life anymore. I had to disappear to protect you."

"Why didn't you take me with you?"

"It was too dangerous! I turned myself in and I worked with a police investigator, helping him to track down the traffic business from Rio to Mexico City. It was the only way I would clean my name.

I had no other choice. But I have always loved you…" Rafael teared up looking straight into her eyes.

She went crazy at him. She turned from a happy drunk to an angry panther.

"You left me on our wedding day, and vanished Rafael! What do you expect now? How do you think I got over everything?" She yelled at him, crying. Then pushed him away; then pulled him back again and hugged him. Jack was crying too.

"I love you. Just come back to me, Mari…" He pressed her body tightly against his. She pulled herself away from him and punched him twice on his chest, then hugged him tight again.

"I hate you so much for everything…" She whispered, hugging him. She couldn't keep herself off his chest.

Then, Mariana's friend came along and pulled her away from Rafael.

"Go back to hell and leave her alone, Rafael! She has a new life now, and a real man by her side. Not a junkie drug dealer like you." She dragged Mariana out of the Parade. Mariana was crying, tripping over, and feeling completely lost.

They walked towards the side street. Mariana could still hear Rafael calling.

"Trust me, Mari! I will never leave you again…" He kept crying out.

"I need a drink of water." She abruptly stopped.

"All right, wait here. I will buy it." Mariana's friend crossed the road to a bar.

When she came back, Mariana had disappeared.

Ipanema Beach. One of the most famous beach of Rio. Place for many Carnaval Parades during February.

BLEEDING FLOWERS

(Cinelandia – Centre of Rio – 1968)

I was there, at the demonstration, in front of the Embassy and I remember thinking: *This is fabulous! I am anti-imperialist. Yes! I am.* My friends and I, we are deeply against dictatorship. We are radical! Not only because they do horrible things, but also because we can't stand these heartless gringos. Disgusting…

It was a remarkable afternoon! Through the waving protest flags, I could see the burning sunset. The last shining orange rays made me feel invincible. I could rise myself up to the sky and touch it. I felt radiant! I was wearing a flowery dress and I had white lilies in my hair. I felt like dancing! So, I spun around with wide opened arms while seeing people marching proudly, satisfied that their voices were finally being heard during the protest. I was bursting with enthusiasm and saying out loud: "This is an extraordinary feeling! This is freedom! We all deserve it!"

Then my eyes spotted him. He was watching me. Just there, a few steps away. Those brilliant smiling green crystals were staring at me. People started shouting "Out, out, out, out, imperialism out" and so did we. Together with our gaze locked on each other, our words became louder and louder "out, out, out, out, imperialism out" and again and again, harmoniously. As the throng moved forward, we were swept closer together until we bumped shoulders. The chanting was powerfully sung within the crowd and I heard him saying to me: "You've inspired my soul! You are delightful to watch!" The heat beaming from my heart could melt an iceberg.

Unexpectedly, the gunfire started. A scene from hell. People running, yelling, trying to escape. The shots were becoming more intense and closer to us. I felt my whole body turn to stone. Voices were silenced from my ears… and just like a scene in slow motion, I saw the bullet merge forcefully through his black hair. Down! He fell like a bird. Not a sound. He didn't even scream. I sat and placed his head on my lap. Instantly, I had bleeding flowers on my dress. For a second, he gasped while the green faded from his eyes. I screamed out "help, please!", but it fell on deaf ears. No one noticed us.

Suddenly, a terrifying silence came about. No more shooting. The world stopped. His last verses were still echoing intensely in my memory. Six dead bodies fallen down on the ground around me. Tragically, he was the seventh.

The next day, the newspaper reported the demonstration. But mentioned nothing about the dead people. They took the bodies away to cover the evidence. They never said a word about the shooting. Those military policemen, monsters' capitalists. No sympathy at all. Have they ever known pain? Why did they shoot? To show the power they think they have? This is not power! This is murder! Dictators inject fear, slay innocent life and strip away our freedom!

I kept my flowery dress stained with the boy's blood in a box with a note assuring him I was going to be present in all of the demonstrations to fight for justice and freedom, for him and for me. I went to another street protest a week after. And to another one the next day. I met other young people who were even more engaged than I was. We met up every Friday at an abandoned shed near the pier. We talked and planned our next actions against the bloody military.

Demonstrations would never fail our dream of being free. I remember in one of the latest protests when we saw military policeman running towards the crowd carrying Molotov cocktail on their hands, we could not help but scream "Fuck the hell out here, coward bastards!" I ran towards one of them and banged his legs with a piece of timber. The man fell over my feet. I kept smashing his body with the timber until he was drowned in his own blood.

Six months later, five friends of mine and I had our faces in every newspaper of Rio. We were the dangerous young people gang wanted by Brazilian Federal Police and FBI for the kidnapping of the U.S Ambassador to Brazil. We did it! We were proud we did it! We would do it all again if necessary. We were members of the MR8 (Revolutionary Movement 8th October) and we were armed resistance to the excruciating military dictatorship.

Building of the City Council of Rio. Many political protests are held in front of the building.

Inspired by the set of events called "Revolution in 1968" that first took place in Paris, France, and later in the same year, in Rio de Janeiro, during the dictatorship political system. People were active participants in demonstrations and protests. Sadly, some of artists, intellectuals and writers were exiled outside Rio and victims of torture. Some others were unfairly assassinated.

THE DEATH OF THE DIRECTOR

(Santa Tereza – Centre of Rio)

Stuck in the dance studio shed
waiting for his death
legs trapped under timber and glass
blood all over the stairs ahead
Director was almost-dead
He feels sorry for his ballerina darling
who will see his body
numb and palid.
She will shake him once and again:
"Director, my love!"
Director then will be in silent,
morbid pain.
Death is not his concern
but his ballerina darling
abandonded, slim
with nothing left of him.
He wants her to know that
the argument of the opening night,
while sleeping outside
under the street lights
only love filled his mind.
But now, death is taking him away
leaving her alone, deserted, stray.
He only hopes
that she can hear
his ghostly words
whispered behind her ears.
My ballerina darling,
don't waste all your tears!

Selaron Stairs in Santa Teresa. Famous art work steps by Chilean Jorge Selaron.

THE CASINO OF LOVE

(Urca – South of Rio – 1920)

Through the bohemian picturesque streets of Urca
Where artists paint and sing nothing else but love

Round playful skirt makes waves with the wind
She walks towards the red casino for love

Gentlemen, businessmen, players all over machines
She walks backstage for the job that brings her love

Red velvet curtains and friendly smiles welcome her in
Dazzling costumes, sequins and feathers announce the dance of love

Jacques Offenbach tunes of the scandalous Cancan begins
Crotch less underpants dancers excite the room with sexual love

She looks the audience and spots the poet, the one and only
Sitting down looking lonely, searching for true love

In a glimpse of contemplation, he smiles at her
The poet and the Casino courtesan fall in inciting love

Jacques Offenbach was the French composer of 'Orpheus in the Underworld' – the music most associated with the famous Cancan dance.

The very charming and unique Urca suburb. The place for the very fist Casino of Rio in the 1900s.

DUET DIALOGUE

(Cinelandia – Teatro Odeon – Centre of Rio)

Dancing is speaking with the body the words one can't say
She exaggerated the form, plies too low, and pirouette démodé
Unbalanced, her body said too much, too loud, astray

The grandiose theatre empty, not audience, just the two of them to play
He tried to hold her, first position arms, fondu, developpe
Dancing is speaking with the body the words one can't say

They practiced and practiced, sweat, blisters, tears away
He leaped, deboule towards her, she replied with a fouette
Unbalanced, her body turned too quick, too vulgar, astray

Again, he tried, and avoided her fall by twisting on her way
She disagreed, battement tendu, arabesque penchee
Dancing is speaking with the body the words one can't say

Exhausted, he still wanted to dance the best duet of their day
Irritated, she went, tombe, pas de bourree, glissade, grand jete
Unbalanced, her body spoke out of beat, too showy, astray

In spite of the time, hard work, attempts and training,
They couldn't get one routine right, one lift steady, one word agreed
Their bodies didn't blend, angry looks crossed the mirror, not gay
She stopped. He gave up. They booked a final rehearsal for the next day.

Plie: *bent;* *Fondu*: *sinking down;* *Developpe*: *developing movement;* *Battement tendu*: *beating leg stretched up, then foot touches the floor;* *Arabesque penchee*: *position supported on one leg straight back up and body leaning all the way down to the floor.* *Tombe*: *fallen;* *Pas de bourree*: *step gliding;* *Glissade*: *glide;* *Grand jete*: *horizontal jump starting from one leg and landing to the other.*

Odeon Theatre. One of the oldest theatre in the city.

LAST LETTER FROM LEBLON

(Leblon – South of Rio – late 90s)

I wonder what you've been up to since you left the neighbourhood, ninety-four days ago. This was supposed to be our place. You moved me here to this so called the finest suburb of Rio, dribbling your discourse that there is no place like Leblon. You made up my mind that here I'd get a job on a theatre stage, go trendy shopping, meet cool artists with brilliant minds. All this crap, for what? I'm without you now. I still miss you. I know I shouldn't, but I miss the beginning of us here in Leblon.

I remember our nights walking drunk at Avenida Delfim Moreira, tripping each other's steps along Leblon beach pathway when you grabbed my hand and made me look at the Vidigal Mountain and promise one summer night we would jump of Niemeyer Road to diving to the ocean below. I remember our first Valentine's Day date at *Marina Hotel,* when I spilt the blend of bitters, gin, and lime juice all over your brand-new Tommy Hilfiger T-shirt. You revenged sticking your fingers inside me from under the table in front of the nice waiter when he brought a cloth to dry your shirt. I never forget our late dinner at *Degrau* when we didn't have money to pay the bill and did a runner like two foolish teenagers. You loved to act like a boy even though you turned forty last year. I still laugh when I remember us sharing mozzarella pizza at *Guanabara* - the stretchy cheese you pulled from my mouth to yours until you made the longest cheese line that would go as far as where you could sit away from me. Silly man! I was so madly in love with you I couldn't even think straight.

But it is our very first date my best memory of you. I remember my heart beating fast when I saw your black Porsche pulling over in front of my old building at Botafogo. I was unsure what perfume to choose, then I looked at my *Victoria Secret's Love Spell* and thought "*Yes, perfect sign.*" Sprayed it all over my body. My hair wasn't dried enough but I thought '*maybe he likes the last-minute shower type of girl.*' My purple skirt didn't match my black boots, but there was no time left to choose another outfit. When I finally got to the footpath, you smiled and said 'you look sexy, babe.' I felt so nervous I tripped on the broken kerbside, and fell right on top of a dog diarrheal poo. 'Oh shit!' I cried. You quickly came to my rescue. "Shit all right!" you said laughing. I was so pissed off I couldn't even smile. The *Love Spell* became shit enchantment. I had to get changed. You insisted to come up. There went all the romance of what could've been the perfect first date.

You couldn't wait until I finish my shower, remember? You came inside the bathroom, picked up my towel, and started drying me. My body tensed with expectation. I was blushing. I couldn't even look at you. You started kissing my neck, my collar. Your lips touched my nipples. Legs trembling. I couldn't stand stable. You lift me up and carried me to bed. I still remember your breathed words right inside my ears 'Relax, babe, I will teach you everything. Just enjoy the ride.' Then you popped a pill inside your mouth and kissed me. My tongue twisted yours. I tasted the sweetness of hell. I was insanely excited. I wanted you to tear my body and penetrate my soul. After that first time, I begged for doses of ecstasy, like a child cries for cotton candies at the park.

I don't miss the things you made me do that fucked me up. Like sucking those damn sweet pills to get high when you wanted to have fun, gulping whisky without the rocks when I was sad, and smoking pot every night before bed because you couldn't fuck without a hit. You were very clever at getting me to act exactly the way you wanted. I'd say 'I don't feel like smoking tonight.' You'd pull your killer comment 'I hadn't realised you were so prissy, babe.' You made my mind a mess, and turned me into an addicted who couldn't even stand up for myself. I hate you for showing me off to your intellectual piece of shit friends as if I was your precious dumb doll. You plunked me among all this shit that never belonged to me.

I'm surviving though. I have been clean for the last four weeks. Exactly twenty- eight days without drinking, being stoned, or getting high. I don't need those gloom days in my life anymore. I stopped making myself miserable. "How the hell can she survive one day without it?" I imagine you saying this out loud, laughing, and shaking your head from side to side holding your cock like you want to take a piss. I hate having these vivid images and memories of you. The way you walk on these streets as if you know everyone, our proud way introducing yourself as a contemporary writer to every producer you meet, your self-righteous talk, your smart-ass middle-aged look, your old pair of ripped Lee jeans smelling your cigarettes. You are an asshole. You eat shit and burp caviar. Why can't I just delete you off my mind? Stop calling me for damn sake! Just stop! I don't need flowers and red wine bottles at my door every fucking weekend. This is close to ridiculous. I'm not your Barbie anymore. Let me be a normal person! You owed me this.

There is nothing you can do to change what you did on that awful night. You ruined me! You fucked that scrawny fake blonde receptionist from the *Copacabana Palace Hotel* at the back of the bar on my 21st birthday party! I still hear your drunk words to me: "Come on Sugar Plum, she is nothing compared to you. I'm a dupe. I'm smashed. Everybody is. I'm too high to make sense of it all, babe …" Yes, you were high, but I was there! I saw you banging that bitch from behind, pulling her brassy yellow hair back, slapping her white potato ass full of cellulite … You pressed her hips against yours, bent your head back, and groaned "I'm coming!" I run away from that pub, in the rain. Spent the night inside *General Osorio - Ipanema* subway station. I woke up the next day, face down on my own vomit. I came back to the apartment and you were gone. Your guilt killed your pride and you had to leave. It sucks that my last memory of you is this sickening one.

Since then, I have been crazy trying to get over you. The absence of the drugs doesn't help, but I need to keep strong. I want to think for my own, to make plans. I want to go back to University and finish my Degree you made me stop saying 'Studying is bullshit babe, a total waste of time.' I need to believe you never really loved me. You loved to control me. But I can't be controlled anymore. Some days, like today, I want to yell at you, punch you on a face, then choke you until your skin lose colour, your mind faint, your eyes droop down, and you die, helpless. Or maybe strike a sharp knife right into your heart and watch you bleed to death. But then, I realize I must let go this exterminator feeling, because I'll never be emotionally able to actually kill you, even if I could. So, I decided to write you this last letter. And so, you know I'm trying everything I can to forget you.

I met a guy two weeks ago. A good one, I guess. He's younger and hotter than you. He came along by surprise and spoke to me on my audition day for Carl's production. I got in, by the way. And I didn't need you to put a good word in. I did it, alone. For the next four months, I have a job. And a new boyfriend. He is in the play too. We see each other every day and spend hours rehearsing. Yesterday, I played the piano for him. Then I felt hungry. He went to the kitchen, opened the cupboard, and reached for the fig jam. He looked at me with a cheeky smile. I was almost certain about what he was thinking. I was still sitting on my piano seat. He brought the jam over and sat on the keyboard in front of me. The sound of the harmony from the C sharp to the F flat echoed in the room. I smiled.

He started feeding me. Indicator finger full of jam right into my mouth. I licked it a little. He licked the rest and dug in for a bit more. I giggled. He moved his body and sounded the G key. My favourite! I asked for more. A jam covered finger again into my mouth. This time, I accidentally bit it. He smiled. I licked the jam around my lips, then got up. He pulled me over to him and kissed the rest of the jam off my lips. Twisted tongues. Sugary. He lifted me to his lap. My legs crossed around him. He pressed me closer. Three fingers traced down under my dress. Slippery. Soaked undies down to the floor. *Mel* dripping down my thighs. He licked his honeyed fingers. Slid down his zipper. Moved my hips a little. Inside. Gentle. Slow. Then rough. Heat. G sharp key echoing. Fast. Faster. Rhythm. Finally, the G higher! Tremor. Ecstasy – the real one.

He takes me to a place sunnier than Leblon. A place where things feel real, safer, where I don't need to pretend to be someone I'm not. I still think about you, but I'm leaving Leblon at the end of this week. I'm moving back to Botafogo where I should never have left. I'm going back to my neighbourhood. The place that reflects who I am. I'll leave behind all the reminiscences of you. The classy cool impression of Leblon you created to me quickly became dark. Unbearable, actually. Leblon became an underworld to me. I hate looking at the Marina Hotel when I drive past it. I used to enjoy living here with you, but your dirty habits stained the charming atmosphere forever. I may never come back.

Leblon beach view from Niemeyer road.

Leblon beach from Arpoador headland

CONFESSIONS OF A PROSTITUTE

(Copacabana – South of Rio)

Tear half of my body
Slash my heart
Wipe off my dreams
Take fragments of me
Anything that makes me break into pieces
Anything that makes me scream!
Slap me on the face
Scratch my old tattoos
Rip all my given expensive clothes
Handcuff me naked on a street post
Kick me hard, anything that gives me pain!
Wakes me up from this dirty life
Can't even call this a life
Every night, another man, a different tourist
Walking on the path of Copacabana beach
A foreign accent
Moans in my ears
White skin, heavy body
Sweats on my tan curved one
I want to vomit
But I need the money!
Take me away from Copacabana
Please, recreate me
Give me a new identity
A decent job, a normal family
A real life
I can't stand not fitting anywhere.

Copacabana Beach. One of the most famous beach in Rio well known by its path design.

THE BEAST

(Lapa – Centre of Rio)

Magali swung the lantern around again and said, "See, there's nothing out there. Don't need to be sacred. What about we sing a song? Take your mind off it."

"Mummy, I'm scared."

Magali held Carla's hand and started to sing *Ciranda-Cirandinha*. Carla's voice trembled with fear as the dense steps came closer and closer. She couldn't understand how her mother seemed unaware to the sound.

Magali's singing grew louder, and up ahead they could see the warm glow of light from their own home shone through the trees of the alleyway behind the Arcs of Lapa monument.

"Carla, see, we're almost home."

"Let's hurry then Mummy. Can't you hear it? It's getting closer!"

"I'm telling you there's nothing there."

Magali made another sweep around with the lantern, then she squeezed Carla's hand and they started running without looking back. They stepped down on the trail to home.

"Magali, is that you?" A familiar voice called.

Magali took a deep breath. Carla smiled as her father's voice came out of the darkness.

"Yes Pedro. I'm sorry we're so late. And tired. We walked a bit fast, then we ran the rest of the way off the track. Carla's worn out."

Pedro picked up his daughter and carried her home. Once inside their small cottage, Magali helped Carla undress and quietly tucked her in bed.

"You are safe now darling. Sleep well." Magali left Carla's bedroom.

Carla smiled and started to pray. She felt thankful and relieved that she and her mother were finally safe at home. Before closing her eyes, she heard her mother's voice coming from the kitchen. She got up, walked to the door. Ears glued to it.

"Pedro, I heard something out there. It sounded like deep steps. I didn't want to frighten Carla. I kept singing and wavering the lantern around, telling her there was nothing to be scared of, but I was scared for both of us."

"What are you talking about woman?" Pedro wasn't giving her much attention. He opened a beer and sat on the couch.

"Listen! I'm telling you there was something out there. Just before we got off the tracks, I turned on the lantern one last time. That's when I saw what was tracking us. I can't be wrong Pedro.

"You girls are hallucinating! I know this is not the safest place to live, but that's all we can afford at the moment.

"It was a strange creature half man and half beast. He looked at the light with furious red eyes. I turned off the lantern, grabbed Carla's hand, and ran." Magali heard a noise coming from Carla's bedroom.

Carla's legs couldn't make her stand steady. Her window cracked opened. She crawled quietly to under her bed and started praying again.

The beast was inside Carla's bedroom. She could hear his respiration and see his big hairy feet walking passed the bed to the door.

He walked rocky, unsteady, to the living room and faced Pedro and Magali. The smell of booze filled the room.

"Hey guys! This Carnaval costume is getting too heavy. I just came from the big parade. I'm a bit drunk, and lost, you see? I followed the girls trying to find a place. Would you mind if I spent the night?"

Arcos da Lapa (Arcs of Lapa). Famous architecture of Rio.

THE GRAND PHANTOM

(Cinelandia – Teatro Municipal - Centro of Rio)

Theatre black curtains wide open
Blue lights spot main stage of the Great Actors theatre
Orchestra loudly plays first tune of *Angel of music*
Prima ballerina dances in her dressing room scenario

Audience awaits in suspense silence
Where is the phantom?
The labyrinth underground setting
Calls for him among scary fog and excitement

Beyond the lake song echoes lurid
The phantom grand and mysterious enters the stage
He is stranger than she dreamed
But he is a fool who makes her laugh

On the white veranda of the central scenario
Phantom and prima ballerina waltz their love
'Why did you bring me here,' she wonders
'You are mine,' he whispers

'Angel of music' and 'Beyond the lake' are famous compositions made for 'The Phantom of the Opera' original musical.

Teatro Municipal. City Public Theatre. The most famous theatre space in the city. House for many dance companies from around the world.

THE SETUP

(Guaratiba – Southwest of Rio – 1980s
– inspired by an old folk tale)

Summer time. Robert, a handsome middle-aged American man, is driving a rental white sedan type of car on an old bumpy road coming back from a work meeting. The windows are open, he feels the wind on his face. Robert loves the tropical weather. He looks at the last ray of sunset. Birds are chirping. Bats flock across the darkening sky.

Bang. The car shudders. Front tyre flaps about on its rims. Robert stops and gets off the car. He examines the front tyre pulling out a piece of timber on which are attached sharp nails. He through it on the side of the road. He opens the boot to get the spare tyre but finds out the spare is totally flat empty. He shuts the boot, upset. He looks around. There are no houses or service station. Robert gets back into the car and rests his head on the steering wheel, unhappy.

Headlights loom up in the dark. Robert gets out of his car tooting and waving.

A rusty Ute approaches slowly laden with crates. The doors are attached to the chassis with bits of rope. Windows open. A good-looking young man, Lucas, is driving. He stops and asks if Robert is in any trouble. Robert tells him the situation. Lucas offers Robert a lift to a mechanic nearby. Lucas is the only help that comes in hand. Robert accepts the lift, picks up the spare tyre, and gets in Lucas's car.

Along the way, Robert - who is very friendly and always open to a fresh friendship - makes ordinary conversation about the hot weather in the tropical country, and the nice hotel he is staying at. Lucas doesn't speak much. He agrees about the hot weather, and smiles. Robert takes a good look at him. Lucas wears ripped jeans and old brown boots. His long hair is tied up, and his beard shaved. Robert looks around inside the car. The seats are a bit worn out. Robert can smell fresh fruit and vegetables from the wooden boxes in the back tray. Lucas tells Robert that before getting to the mechanic, he has to stop, a few kilometres out of the road, to deliver the wooden boxes.

They stop at a deserted large property with a small shack and an old shed at the back. The shack is old and small. There are palings of wood missing and some windows are cracked. Sepia lights are seen on the inside and bright ones at the veranda where wooden colourful bird's decorations are hanging out. Lucas turns off the car. They get out of the car. Robert looks around while Lucas starts unloading the boxes. A tired looking dog accompany an old toothless lady, Mrs. Mendes. She approaches Robert and, very welcoming, introduces herself as Mrs. Mendes, Lucas's mother. Mrs. Mendes, a humble, old lady, has a strong personality, and very courteous manners towards Robert. She invites him to stay for dinner emphasizing she makes the tastiest stew in town. Robert politely refuses the invite saying he is only waiting for Lucas to finish unloading the car.

Lucas finishes dropping the boxes and tries to start the car, but the motor sounds dead. He tries again to no avail. Mrs. Mendes, claiming it to be destiny, tells Robert he is staying the night, and having the juiciest stew of his life. Robert finds himself in an uncomfortable situation and has no other option but to stay. Mrs. Mendes pulls a strident laugh that disturbs Robert a little bit by the fact that her mouth lacks most of her teeth.

Around the small rectangular timber dining table, Mrs. Mendes is sitting on the headboard. Lucas is on her right side and Robert in front of her. Robert feels relax and contented. He says he likes their hometown and he is very grateful for having met such caring people. Mrs. Mendes thanks him for being a kind guest. Then she calls someone by the name of Celia. Robert is surprised that someone else lives in that out-of-the-way house. Celia, a strikingly beautiful young lady, enters the dining room carrying a large clay pot to the table. Robert stares at her. Celia is wearing an old short dress, letting show an appealing pair of tan legs. She places the clay pot on the table. Robert has a hint of her impeccable round breasts. He is bothered by her gorgeousness.

Robert is adoring Celia's delightful presence at dinner. She licks her lips every now and then, while gazing at Robert. He is enjoying the succulent stew, but sometimes he is bothered by Mrs. Mendes's toothless mouth. While she eats, Robert sees pieces of meat being crushed by her gums. The little amount of food left in her mouth mixes with the lot of saliva forming drools that trickles down her chin and drops on the table. She cleans up with the table cloth.

After dinner, Mrs. Mendes shows Robert the bedroom he is staying the night in. It is a small bedroom with an out-fashioned timber widow bed covered by an antiquated bed spread. Robert is sitting on the bed. He grabs his wallet of his pocket, pulls out a family photo of him, his wife and small daughter. He kisses the photo and pulls it back into the wallet. He places his wallet back into his pocket and looks around. He realizes a common door linking to another bedroom. He looks at the common door, and notices a crack in it. He immediately gets up and spies what's on the other side.

Celia is standing back to the door. She takes her dress off letting it fall slowly down, through her curvilinear body, to the floor. Robert sees she is wearing a tiny white G-string undies. She bends over, reaches the dress, grabs it off the floor, and hangs it on a nail on the wall. She is now too close to the common door. Robert walks away from the door, and paces agitated back and forth in his bedroom. He looks again through the crack.

Celia is now naked, lying in bed, hands between her thighs, playing with herself. Robert urgently takes off his pants. He is turned on. Suddenly, she opens the common door. He is naked and amazed. He instantly pulls her naked body against his, and kisses her voraciously. She sucks his mouth and scratches his back. Then she jumps on him, legs around his hips. He walks to bed carrying her, and lie on top of her. Celia grabs his shoulders, pushes him away and lies him back down in bed. She sits on him. They have a night of lust and madness. Celia dominates sex unlike anyone else he has ever been with. He has the ultimate night of his life.

The next morning, Robert wakes up alone in bed. He gets dressed and leaves the room. Mrs. Mendes is in the kitchen cooking something Robert says it smells unusual but delicious. She tells him it is fresh batch bacon that she carved it up herself three days ago. Robert notices a massive knife in her apron belt, and an empty clay pot beside cuts of vegetables. He goes outside to look for Celia but can't find her. He wanders into the shed.

The shed has a big stained worn out wooden table in the middle, putrid boxes stacked on the floor, and different sized knives and blades lined on the walls. Lucas creepily appears in the doorway, hands behind his back, and asks Robert if he enjoyed penetrating Celia the night before. While Robert is stammering an apology, Lucas advances on him and pulls a machete from behind his back. He swings it at Robert but misses. They tussle on the floor. Lucas gets up and is ready to kick Robert on the face. Robert quickly trips Lucas's other leg. Lucas hits his head on the table edge and falls back on the floor. He's bleeding.

Robert runs out of the shed. Old dog barks at him. He keeps running towards the brushwood. As he enters the bush, he sees cuts of human body parts on the ground. Flies hove. The smell is putrid. Robert wants to vomit. Two wild dogs are eating the remains. They look spot Robert and bark angrily at him, drooling. Robert runs back. One of the dogs gets to his legs and bits it, tossing it. Robert falls down. Dog keeps biting his leg. He manages to kick the dog with his other leg. Still on the ground, he gets a thick stick and hits the dog's head. He gets up, and runs out of the bush towards the dirt road, limping. He is sweating and tired. He looks towards where he came from the night before. He walks to that direction.

Robert walks disoriented. He is limping, his leg hurts. The sun shines right on his eyes. He looks sad and tired. A car approaches him. It is Celia. She drives slowly beside him saying she is not related to that people; she only works in the kitchen. Robert keeps walking. She tells him Lucas came for her too and she needs to escape. Robert stops. She says they need to get to the police station, and tells him to get in the car. As Robert is rounding the vehicle to get to the passenger seat, she runs him over. She reverses the car, and verifies Robert is badly hurt but still alive. She ties Robert's arms to the back of the car with a rope, and his legs to one another. Robert's body is facing the sun. Blood is dripping through his head and eyes. Celia gets the piece of wood with nails on it, and places it on the road. Robert watches her, devastated. She gets back into the car, and drives back home, dragging Robert along.

Back at the property, Celia parks the car outside the shed. Lucas comes and helps her to untie Robert's arms. His legs are still tied up together. They drag Robert to the shed, put him on the table. Robert is awfully injured. Mrs. Mendes comes in wearing her apron and surgical gloves. She places the clay pot on the shed bench, and picks up the best blade from the wall. She pulls a terrifying laugh. Robert sees the blade heading for his head. He blacks out. She strikes the major cut. Blade cutting strident noise echoes out.

At that night, another man stops with a flat tyre. He gets off his car and sees the woody piece with nails on it. Headlights loom up in the dark.

Barra de Guaratiba lake view

THE EVIL WEATHER

(Arpoador – South of Rio)

The eye of a storm spots it
Nose of the mountain smells it
Tongue of the wind announces it
River's mouth opens discussion
What do we do with the evil weather?

Neck of the woods turns against it
Bone of the trunk feels strong for it
All of the tree arms embrace any idea
And fingers lake type question
What do we do with the evil weather?

The ear of the dirt listens
Foothill is invited to step in
Headwaters think straight
We are going to nurse the evil,
Embrace it, love it, and welcome it

Unhappy, round face sun hides behind curved dark hip clouds
Mid-afternoon leg rain inundates the unsettled green ground
Evil weather, crazy, runs past

Relieved, twilight body sky appears
Fingernail moon arrives
Diamond starts sing
And the elegant silhouette night
Makes peaceful Arpoador tonight

Arpoador Beach view from Arpoador point.

AT JOAQUINA BAR

(Leme – South of Rio)

She was sitting alone at *Joaquina Bar* table two
sipping a cocktail drink, waiting for who knows who

Lost brown eyes in faraway rooms
mind full of regrets, she looks a gloom

The waiter asks for her order but she shakes a 'no'
sips her coffee hinting him to go

A black car stops and an elegant man walks right in
he looks around and spots her with a fling

She sips her drink and gawks at him
He pulls the chair and sits slim

He seems a stranger, not friend, not lover
If once he was, now it's all over

He brings a paper without a cue
She grabs a pen and signs askew

He keeps the paper, gets up and goes
She calls the waiter and order pistachios.

GENEROSITY

(Sao Conrado – South West of Rio)

She is generous
She cooks hot meals
for the homeless family
who lives down the road
when she sees the family
she hands them the meals gently
one at a time
starting with the two kids
she moves her hands
like a fairy using her wand
like dancing with in the wind
she lives in a stunning
three bedrooms apartment
facing the beach
in a 14 metres high building in Sao Conrado
a sad contrast between
the fortunate people who can afford a decent life
and the ones who just gets by
sleeping on cardboards
just 46 feet below

AT TWILIGHT

(Tijuca – North of Rio)

Walking at twilight I found an owl
Injured down by the kerbside at Ladislau Neto Street.
It was dangerous to leave her in that corner:
night is falling, another car could turn straight into her.

Looking at her eyes I felt the pain of her insides
I gently touched her fragile feathery body;
she made a noise, strident vocal pleading for aid.
I picked her up; she blinked in appreciation.

Holding her in warm arms I heard a growl—
she looked at me, her body shaking
I saw the shadow of her other foe.
Coming from the back street, he barked drooling in hunger.

Our eyes stared, mine, the black rottweiler, the owl
under the darkening sky, in agony - my only thought –
one of us wins the unfair dispute.
The stillness around us, a waiting audience.

I stood still facing the dog – the panic ruled –
without hesitation, I slowly bowled the owl to him.

THE HILL

(Vidigal – South of Rio)

Some summer mornings
she used to walk up
her favourite hill
she sat down on the rock
facing the Leblon beach
and watch the town wake up
she used to sit and eat jaboticaba berries
from the very old
jaboticaba tree
that has a thin trunk
some other trees had thicker trunks
like the almond tree across from her house
from the rock she could see
the street lights turned off
cars waking up their engines
the man jogging
and the old lady carrying the fresh bread
the hill was nobody's place
but hers when she was there
during summer
the wind refreshed her mind
helped her forget things
to breathe and refeed herself
with hope

BEFORE

(Jacarepagua – West of Rio)

I wish we could wake up
to when we were before

when we were
$\qquad$ something yet to begin

to when that star fell off the sky
and we saw it
$\qquad$ together

to when we were everything
to when we laughed
we were brave, full of life
$\qquad$ and love

I wish we could just wake up
To when we were before

before everything exploded
$\qquad$ and we became who we are now

before the noise
the chaos

I wish
we could only wake up
$\qquad$ before

Barra da Tijuca waters viewed from Jacarapagua suburb

ECCENTRIC THEATRE

(Jardim Botanico – South of Rio)

In a midsummer day, Shakespeare
twittered his whole company
calling for a meeting at the Theatre and Technology Fair
held at Jardim Botanico in Rio.
His latest inspiration would put together
Blu-Ray, Bluetooth, iPhones, iPads and Androids
as obsoletes characters in a future
where electricity was earned by great talent
Peter Quince, the carpenter,
who now is a famous builder,
brought his iPad
Nick Bottom, the weaver,
who became a magnificent artist,
held proudly his iPhone 7
Robin Starveling, the tailor,
who designed the previous Rio Fashion,
made sure his Samsung 9 was turned on
Tom Snout, the tinker,
and Snug, the joiner,
both partners at Apple supplies store,
took along new iPads for all of them.
Francis Flute, the bellows-mender,
was already at the Fair,
as he is now the creator
of Techno Theatre versus Nature Theatre,
something Shakespeare has been willing
to make in 3D for a long time.

Jardim Botanico. Botanical Gardens of Rio. It shows the diversity of Brazilian and foreign flora.

HERE, HELP YOURSELF

(Botafogo – South of Rio)

Here, the photo album of my sophomore year,
me, two years later touring in Argentina,
Guevara, giving his speech of freedom.

Here, there is salmon we can cook,
brown rice we can boil,
and a bottle of white pinot noir we can share.

Here, I let you do the dishes
enjoy the luxury of my sheets,
and maybe kiss my lips.

Here, I teach you how
to make an origami,
and to go to sleep without sex.

Here, read my favourite book
it's about a girl who isn't afraid of heights,
nor is scared of darkness.

Here, listen to my stories and my songs,
understand my syntax
and the poems I write

Here, help yourself
on knowing me, respecting me,
then, and only then, I might love you.

Botafogo suburb. The view from a building apartment.

ILLUSION

(Barra da Tijuca – South West of Rio)

Among all the things in the world
there is only one I would like you to give me:
An illusion.

An illusion that could make lighter to carry
all the impossibilities in between us.
An illusion that could ease the pain
built in my chest because of you.

An illusion that could take me everywhere.
An illusion made by sparse clouds
that brings the inexorable rain
of summer afternoons.

An illusion that could announce a date
for us to meet once in a while.
An illusion that could book a trip
for us to take on the next holidays.

An illusion that could bring news about you
that could give me logic sense,
to understand the affection my heart
insists to feel about you.

An illusion that would give me a hat
to magic you instead and give me the idea of a life
I imagine to be real
or I will possibly die.

THE EMPTY BOAT

(Recreio – Southwest of Rio)

The harder I try to remember
the more it fades into blurry memory
of that day with him
We were in a timber row boat
I remember thinking how strong
he was being able to row
I remember my fascination with
how sunrays travel through the water
in shafts of light, down deep
beyond my vision
giving me an eerie fear
of the unknown

Then, he was gone

I yelled for help
No one heard me
I couldn't swim
I found the strength
to row back alone
licking my salty tears

His head shot
is glued at the police station's
missing person's wall

I still see the empty boat

THINKING OF YOU

(Ipanema – South of Rio)

It's Friday night
around 10:30

I'm reading
Bolton's poem

the one that feels
like 'Talking to You'

he's at his desk
(I'm at mine)

feeling a bit under the weather
despite the full moon

he's drinking the
very last of his bourbon

I don't have a bottle
of bourbon at the moment

but I remember when
you brought me one

the night you decided
to tell me about your fears

when you got me drunk
took me to bed

and fucked me
without taking off

my peach dress
the one

you gave me
for my birthday

in this poem of Bolton
he talks about

the poems
he might write

and if he will ever get
a bourbon for his birthday again

will I ever get
another dress for my birthday?

I'm thinking of you
now because

after that night
many, many years ago

I only saw you
once more

before you disappeared
at Bill Cunningham corner

Fifth Ave and 57th St intersection
never felt so empty

where I cried
on my knees

after the argument
you started and then ran off

was this
self-pity?

if I asked you

you would say
I was acting

well
I was not

and I had to
pick up my broken pieces

pull them together
and walk away

alone

but why am I
thinking of you?

Queen's CD is playing now
'Love of My Life'

and I remember
we used to listen to

yes 'you hurt me,
you broke my heart'

I remember
Mercury's death

then Bowie's
and Prince's

and the silenced
tune in my voice

our best collection
is dead

Why aren't you
dead?

if you were
dead

I wouldn't be writing
you this poem

I'd be talking to you
by your grave

on my peach
dress

but once you
are still around

I can offer me
the honour

to feel a little
'intellectual'

and write to you
a poem

I could write
a lot of shit about you

but I want this to sound
like that Sunday morning

at Central Park
where you shameless

proposed to me
without a ring

and to think of all the rings
you didn't answer

the cries
you didn't care

the words
you didn't listen

well, it's over
long time

and this is
just a poem

I must end it
now

because if
I   leave it

I might ~~delete~~ it later
and I can't

I must find the
last line

are you
thinking of me?

Full moon view from an apartment building in Ipanema.

GOING HOME

(Gloria – Centre of Rio – 1930s)

She leaves the house, carrying a dark red leather luggage and a small handbag. She is wearing the perfect tan colour coat for an autumn weather. It was 1941. Another war has begun and she has decided to end her own. She has left a two pages letter for Marcos. She made sure no essential words were left out. She sliced her heart open in explaining her reasons. The ones he would never understand. She walked by the river and remembered the many times she wanted to make everything silence, to cool down her incandescent feelings for her girlfriend Susan. But today, she passed the river in the direction of the train station. She has decided for once and all to find her home, where her heart belongs to. She must go. Petropolis and Susana were expecting her at 2pm. The train window framed the busy city landscape she had to escape. The quiet town is the ticket for her freedom. Susana is the one for love. She is now going home.

Leopoldina train carriage from early 1930s. Nowadays located in Petropolis Rio state.

CHURCH

(Carioca – Centre of Rio)

I'm not going to church today
I know it's Sunday
But it's summer
The beach is getting busy
Colourful umbrellas shade tan bodies
Sand castles make landscape sculptures
I'm not going to church today
I know it's Sunday
But it's summer
The heat is taking up the mercury drip
It's 38 degrees Celsius on the fridge thermometer
And it's still eight in the morning
I'm not going to church today
I know it's Sunday
But it's summer
My heart is full of happiness
My ears hear sounds of music
My body wants to dance
I trust God will understand
I'm not going to church today

Sao Francisco de Paula Church. At Sao Francisco de Paula Plaza in the center zone of Rio. One of the most beautiful churches inside and out.

SAFE HAVEN

(Catete – Centre of Rio)

I remember arriving here a year ago
running from that sound
the agitation
echo of desperation
torment
screams I couldn't confine anymore
in the middle of the chaos the fire started
sepia photos burning brown and yellow
removing our faces away
the house falling apart
breaking spaces of silence
turning quiet rooms into cries of hell
he was still there looking at me
smirking
waiting to see me turn into ashes
suddenly came a void
stillness
the dark
I must have been dead
when a hand pulled me out of heaven
now I only remember arriving in this place
where birds make the sound, I have forgotten
where trees shade my skin
where I belong and he does not
where he will never find me
I finally landed on my safe haven

Gardens of Catete Palace in Catete suburb of Rio. House for Brazil's President Getulio Vargas.

RIO 40 GRAUS

(A non-fiction piece to celebrate the city)

Every summer, an outburst of heat sweeps down from the North to the South of Brazil, along the East coast. It starts in Marajo Island - the most Northern tropical part of Brazil and the closest to the Equator - and it keeps blowing down South, striking hard every state in the Northeast and Southeast with the highest temperature easily reaching 40 Degrees Celsius during the hottest days. The heat finally hits Rio de Janeiro at the beginning of November when, scientifically, it is still the end of spring.

The city meets the early summer, and its people welcome the most euphoric period of the year, a time when people experience all five human senses at once. The early summer fills Rio with exotic flavours of seasonal tropical fruits and spiced ice-creams, the smells from the fishy, salty sea breeze stick to bodies and hairs, the blue colour of the immaculate morning sky shines until the orange-pink perfect sunset at twilight, and the samba drumming mixed with street dance music echoes from every corner. Rio becomes the most exciting city in the world to visit in summer.

Cariocas – the people born in Rio – commemorate this early summer season episode with 'Rio 40 Graus' cultural event, or 'Rio 100 Degrees F.' It is a festive occasion in the city where musicians, poets, painters, writers, and artists in general participate in a series of cultural happenings around the city in order to welcome the early summer and celebrate the people of Rio. Cultural activities inundate the city with creative, transformative, and innovative forms of art. Week nights and weekends are sealed with all sorts of artistic movements.

The streets of Cinelandia, in the centre of Rio, are packed with people listening and dancing to live music concerts. Metro stations, in the South of Rio, stage underground socially engaging theatre plays and poetry recitals with actors walking around the platforms and inside the trains wearing characters costumes, acting out their lines. City art exhibitions, artistic sand sculptures, and live human statues are seen along Ipanema and Copacabana well-known tourist beaches. Incredibly appetizing street food degustation takes place along parks. Ultimately, the people of Rio celebrate themselves dancing around the restaurant and bar tables at Lapa, in the centre of Rio. Also partying under marquees and bamboo gazebos around the coconut trees in Lagoa Rodrigo de Freitas, one of the most fascinating post-cards of Rio.

'Rio 40 Graus' event has always been inspired by the semi-documentary film called *Rio 40 Graus* (1955) wrote and directed by the Brazilian film-maker Nelson Pereira dos Santos. The film shows one Sunday in the life of a few teenagers from favelas, or hillside poor towns, selling peanuts in the tourist places such as Copacabana beach, Sugar Loaf Mountain, and the famous Maracanã soccer stadium, confronting the difference of social class. The story explores the contrast between the distressed life of the poor, the comfortable life of the middle class, and the wealth of the high class in Rio, from the characters' point of view. The movie was the first ever to cover poverty as a social issue in Rio. It was a mark in the Brazilian cinema and in the Rio's culture.

Another inspiration for 'Rio 40 Graus' was a song with the same name composed in 1992 by Brazilian song writers Fausto Fawcett and Carlos Laufer, and singer Fernanda Abreu. The song was recorded in the album *Sla 2 Be Sample* (1992), by Abreu. *Rio 40 Graus* (1992) is the precursor of funk style music in Rio. The lyrics reference the city summer's main occurrences such as high temperatures, mixing of people from different social classes, tourists in the city, cultural expressions within realistic social aspects, violence on the streets, and the city's natural beauty. The first verse of the song resonates brilliantly the face of Rio: "Marvellous city, purgatory of the beauty and the chaos." (Abreu and Fawcett, 1992, verse 1). Singer Fernanda Abreu had energized the people of Rio singing her song in many stage concerts around Rio, such as Copacabana beach and Cinelandia, in the centre of the city. When she came on and the music started, people set off clapping to the rhythm, dancing to the funk steps and singing along out loud with her. Electrifying! A contagious moment that stayed in the Rio's memory of summer, forever.

'Rio 40 Graus' ends by the beginning of December, however the summer remains, moving people's hearts and bodies all the way through Christmas with family gatherings, and New Year's most expected celebration called *Reveillon* at *Copacabana* beach. Cariocas and tourists are all dressed up in white, representing the sentiment of peace and hope for the coming year. February arrives and it means Carnival. During the whole month, people are in the partying fun mood, looking for masks and costumes to wear during the street parades, gathering everywhere, practicing the songs that will take part in the biggest music, lyrics, dance, and costume contest of the year: The Schools of Samba Performing Arts Competition at Sambodromo Avenue, the longest avenue built specially for the event. Carnival in Rio only takes four nights and five days, however the preparations and expectation, and the post-event celebrations of the competition's results can last until the end of March. Cariocas then farewell the Carnival festivities.

Although it is officially the end of the exultant season, the feeling of summer in Rio stays with its people throughout the year. It is endless! Summer in Rio is an experience people can't live without and can't let die. It's a blend of sensations. It's hot and humid, making our short dresses stick to the back of our tights when we get off our seats. It's tumultuous, passionate, musical and noisy during parties when cariocas bump shoulders, dance and sing together. At the same time, summer in Rio holds opposite but still pleasant feelings. Cariocas love the cool and relaxing afternoons after a thunderstorm sitting at the verandas, sipping on a refreshing home-made fruit cocktail. It's also silent when the night arises and people are fulfilled with the pleasure of a perfect day spent in the impeccable city.

This feeling of contentment stays with people all year round. Summer in Rio means inspiration, celebration of culture, belief in people's greatness, happiness, and a willing to look at life with curious eyes and open hearts.

Christ Redeemer. The most famous monument of Rio and also one of the seven wonders of the world.

RIO

Rio of my birth
Rio of my family
Rio of my home
Rio of my heart

Rio that spoke to me
Rio that told me stories
Rio that sang me a song
Rio that opened the curtains

Rio you cheered me up
Rio you applauded my act
Rio you published my name
Rio you carried my dreams

Rio is the sound
Rio is the light
Rio is the green and the blue
Rio is all the colors that are bright

Rio never silent
Rio never dies
Rio always noise
Rio always life

GRANDMA'S HOUSE

(Tijuca – North of Rio)

Front door always open
Family stayed, friends visited, neighbors called in
I was never alone at Grandma's house

Kitchen always noisy
Sound of knifes, stirred spoons, clash of pans
I was never alone at Grandma's house

Dining table always busy
Grandpa talking, uncle coughing, aunty laughing
I was never alone at Grandma's house

Bedroom always full
Rag dolls, pink dresses, red bows
I was never alone at Grandma's house

Verandah always welcoming
Grandma chatting, a friend guffawing, the owl hooting
I was never alone at Grandma's house

HUMMUS AND HERBS

(Alessandra Salisbury's third prize winning
poem at Fusion Poetry Competition at Southern
Cross University – Australia - 2016)

Born in Lebanon, Grandpa sang
only the chorus of an Arabic song.
Born in Italy, Nana spoke
a dialect from Sicily no one understood.

Birth countries left behind,
identities lost in the sea.
Big ship sailed the Atlantic,
in the direction of the east coast of Brazil.

Born fifty years later
in a house full of sound and smells,
I learnt laughter, spoken feelings
Mum and Dad danced the samba well.

Italian hot sauces burnt my tongue,
chick peas and garlic made my taste.
My family taught me to cook, to eat
To travel, to love, and not to miss.

Australia has me now,
Baggage bursting three cultures inside.
In a land of so many immigrants,
Italians and Lebanese sure easy to find.

CPSIA information can be obtained
at www.ICGtesting.com
Printed in the USA
BVHW020904120819
555661BV00007B/78/P